Medieval World

Places of Worship
in the Middle Ages

Kay Eastwood

Crabtree Publishing Company

www.crabtreebooks.com

Crabtree Publishing Company

www.crabtreebooks.com

PMB 16A, 350 Fifth Avenue
Suite 3308
New York, NY 10118

612 Welland Avenue
St. Catharines
Ontario, Canada
L2M 5V6

73 Lime Walk
Headington
Oxford 0X3 7AD
United Kingdom

Coordinating editor: Ellen Rodger

Series editor: Carrie Gleason

Designer and production coordinator: Rosie Gowsell

Scanning technician: Arlene Arch-Wilson

Art director: Rob MacGregor

Project development, editing, photo editing, and layout:
First Folio Resource Group, Inc.: Erinn Banting, Tom Dart,
Jaimie Nathan, Debbie Smith, Anikó Szocs

Photo research: Maria DeCambra

Prepress and printing: Worzalla Publishing Company

Consultants: Isabelle Cochelin, University of Toronto; Joseph
Goering, Department of History, University of Toronto; S. Irtiza
Hasan, Muslim Students Association at the University of Houston

Photographs: Paul Almasy/Corbis/magmaphoto.com: p. 18 (top);
Archivo Iconografico, S.A./Corbis/magmaphoto.com: p. 16, p. 20, p.
29 (top); Art Archive/Biblioteca Nazionale Turin/Dagli Orti: p. 10
(bottom); Art Archive/Bibliothèque des Arts Décoratifs Paris/Dagli
Orti: p. 11 (top); Art Archive/Bodleian Library Oxford/Add A185
folio 106v: p. 8 (right); Art Archive/Bodleian Library Oxford/Arch
Selden A 5 folio 2v: p. 22 (top); Art Archive/Bodleian Library
Oxford/Canon Or 79 folio 2v: p. 22 (bottom); Art Archive/British
Library/Royal 18 D.II: p. 13 (top); Art Archive/Dagli Orti: p. 26 (top);
Art Archive/Museum of Islamic Art Cario/Dagli Orti: p. 24 (top); Art
Archive/Nationalmuseet Copenhagen Denmark/Dagli Orti; Art
Archive/San Francesco Assisi/Dagli Orti: p. 4; Bettman/Corbis/
magmaphoto.com: p. 31 (right); Bibliothèque Nationale, Paris,
France/Bridgeman Art Library: p. 24 (bottom); British Library/Cotton

Nero E. II pt.1 f.73: p. 17 (bottom); British Library, London,
UK/Bridgeman Art Library: p. 23 (right); British Library/Topham-
HIP/Image Works: p. 8 (left), p. 9, p. 28; Mary Evans Picture Library:
p. 7 (top); Giraudon/Art Resource, NY: title page, p. 6, p. 21 (top); E.
Grasset/Mary Evans Picture Library: p. 11 (bottom); Illustrated
London News Picture Library, London, UK/Bridgeman Art Library: p.
10 (top); Wolfgang Kaehler/Corbis/magmaphoto.com: p. 31 (left);
Erich Lessing/Art Resource, NY: p. 19 (bottom); Christophe Loviny/
Corbis/magmaphoto.com: p. 30; Museo Nationale, Rome, Italy/
Bridgeman Art Library: p. 13 (bottom); Richard T. Nowitz/
Corbis/magmaphoto.com: p. 27 (top); Vittoriano Rastelli/
Corbis/magmaphoto.com: p. 27 (bottom); Scala/Art Resource, NY: p.
7 (bottom), p. 12, p. 18 (bottom), p. 21 (bottom), p. 29 (left); Matthew
Turner/Art Directors and TRIP: p. 23 (bottom); Sandro
Vannini/Corbis/magmaphoto.com: p. 17 (top), p. 26 (bottom);
Victoria & Albert Museum, London, UK/Bridgeman Art Library: p. 25

Illustrations: Jeff Crosby: pp. 14–15; Katherine Kantor: flags, title
page (border), copyright page (bottom); Margaret Amy Reiach:
borders, gold boxes, title page (illuminated letter), copyright page
(top), contents page (all), pp. 4-5 (timeline), page 5 (all), page 19
(top), page 32 (all)

Cover: Shortly after birth, a Christian baby was baptized, while
another Christian receives the sacrament of communion.

Title page: Before the 1100s, marriages were private celebrations
held at home. They were not religious ceremonies. Around 1140,
marriages began to be celebrated at the church, in front of a
priest, or a bishop in the case of great nobles.

Published by
Crabtree Publishing Company

Copyright © **2004 CRABTREE PUBLISHING COMPANY.**
All rights reserved. No part of this publication may be
reproduced, stored in a retrieval system or transmitted in
any form or by any means, electronic, mechanical,
photocopying, recording, or otherwise, without the prior
written permission of Crabtree Publishing Company.

Cataloging-in-Publication Data
Eastwood, Kay.
    Places of worship in the Middle Ages / writer by Kay Eastwood.
        p. cm. -- (Medievel worlds series)
Includes index.
Contents: In the Middle Ages -- The church and daily life -- Churches --
Feast days -- Pilgrimages -- A gothic cathedral -- Building a cathedral
-- Christian art -- Monasteries and convents -- Judaism -- Islam -- Mosc
-- The church's influence -- Religion around the world.
  ISBN 0-7787-1347-4 (RLB) -- ISBN 0-7787-1379-2 (pbk)
 1. Religions--History--To 1500--Jovenile literature. 2. Church history--
Middle Ages, 600-1500--Juvenile literature. [1. Church history--Middle
Ages, 600-1500. 2. Religions--History--To 1500] I. Title. II. Series.
  BL97.E25 2003
  200'.9'02--dc22
                                                          2003018229
                                                          LC

Table of Contents

In the Middle Ages

The period from 500 A.D. to 1500 A.D. is known as the Middle Ages, or the medieval period. During this time, kings in western Europe ruled large kingdoms, merchants bought gold, silks, and spices from faraway lands, and towns and cities grew. The Middle Ages was also a time of battles, disease, and famine.

Belief in religion helped people deal with the hardships in their lives. Most people in medieval Europe were Christians. Their religion, Christianity, began about 500 years before the start of the Middle Ages. Christians believe in one God and follow the teachings of Jesus Christ, who they believe is God's son on earth. Today, there are many denominations, or kinds, of Christianity, but in the Middle Ages the Roman Catholic Church was the only Christian Church in western Europe.

▼ *Catholics believe that the pope, who is the leader of the Catholic Church, is God's representative on Earth. Here, a pope speaks to friars, or educated men who traveled from town to town in the Middle Ages preaching God's word.*

Christianity spreads through Europe and becomes the main religion	Muslims conquer Jerusalem	First Romanesque cathedral built	Construction of first Gothic cathedral begins	Jews expelled from England	Formation of Spanish Inquisition
300	642	1000s	1160s	1290	1478

	Muhammad, a prophet of Islam, is born	Muslims conquer Spain	Crusades to the Holy Land begin	Inquisition formed to find heretics	Jews expelled from France	
	570	711	1095	1200s	1300s	

LEGEND
CHRISTIAN LANDS
MUSLIM LANDS
AREA WITH LARGE JEWISH POPULATION

▲ Christianity was not the only religion in the Middle Ages. Some Europeans were Jews. Their religion, Judaism, was thousands of years old. Other people in countries around the Mediterranean Sea followed a religion called Islam, which began in the early Middle Ages.

Dioceses and Parishes

Christian Europe was divided into regions, called dioceses, that a bishop led. Each diocese was divided into smaller regions, called parishes, which had their own churches and priests. This system is still used today. In the Middle Ages, bishops often came from powerful **noble** families and helped priests teach Christianity to the people.

The Catholic Church was wealthy and powerful in the Middle Ages. Bishops and **archbishops** advised kings and the great lords who ruled Europe. The Church also owned large areas of land, and popes, archbishops, and bishops lived like kings in their own palaces.

◀ *King*

◀ *Great lords*

◀ *Lesser nobles*

◀ *Knights*

◀ *Peasants*

▶ *For much of the Middle Ages, kings and great lords were the most powerful people in society, but there were times when the Church was as powerful. Peasants, who farmed the land, had the least power.*

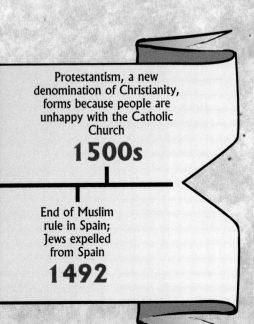

Protestantism, a new denomination of Christianity, forms because people are unhappy with the Catholic Church

1500s

End of Muslim rule in Spain; Jews expelled from Spain

1492

The Church and Daily Life

I n the Middle Ages, religion was a very important part of people's lives. Christians believed that God always watched them. If good things happened, they thanked God for his kindness. If they suffered, they prayed to God for his help.

Christians in the Middle Ages thought that if they followed the teachings of the Bible, the Christian holy book, they would join God in heaven after they died. If they died without being forgiven for their **sins**, they would be sent to a terrible place called hell where **devils** would **torture** them forever.

Christians believed that people who died before they were forgiven for their sins had to spend time in a place called purgatory before going to heaven. Their family and friends said prayers, had the priest say special **Masses**, lit candles, and went on religious journeys called pilgrimages to shorten their stay in purgatory and make sure that they reached heaven. When wealthy people died, they often left the Church land or money to pay for prayers that would help them get to heaven.

▲ *Churches and religious books had paintings of hell to remind Christians not to sin. Hell was ruled by a former angel named Lucifer whom God threw out of heaven. Lucifer is also called Satan.*

Religion and Diet

The Church encouraged people in the Middle Ages to behave in certain ways. For example, people were encouraged to fast on Wednesdays, Fridays, Saturdays, and on the evening before certain religious holidays. On fast days, Christians were supposed to eat only one small meal, and they were not allowed to eat meat, only fish. They also had to fast for the 40 days before Easter, the holiday that marked Jesus' death and his resurrection, or return to life. This fast was called Lent.

▶ *Wealthy people often had private chapels in their homes where they worshiped using books that had prayers and religious stories. These books were written in whatever language the people spoke, instead of the Latin of the Bible, which only educated priests knew how to read.*

Helping Others

The Church helped Christians in their daily lives. It ran most of the schools and hospitals in the Middle Ages and gave alms, or donations of food and clothing, to the poor. To pay for these services and for the local priest, all Christians paid taxes, called tithes, to the Church. The tithe was one tenth of the money or food that a person earned or produced each year.

Churches

Christians pray in buildings called churches, which they consider God's houses on earth. Most churches in the Middle Ages were made of stone and were the largest buildings in the village or town after the castle, if there was one.

The church was the center of religious life. People went there to pray, especially on Sundays, which was considered God's day. The most important part of the Mass was the celebration of the Eucharist. During the celebration of the Eucharist, the priest said a prayer over wine and special bread, called the host. Medieval Christians believed that this blessing turned the wine and bread into the blood and body of Jesus Christ.

▲ *Funeral services for great nobles were held in large cathedrals. A noble's body was buried beneath the cathedral floor and marked with an engraved stone.*

Confession

Christians in the Middle Ages visited the Church to confess, or tell the priest about their sins, and ask for God's forgiveness. Medieval Christians believed that if they sinned too much, they would not get into heaven. The priest gave out punishments, called penances, to wipe away the sin. Penances could be simple, such as saying a certain number of prayers, or difficult, such as having to eat only bread and water or going on a difficult pilgrimage.

◀ *In the Middle Ages, the parish priest was not only a religious leader, but also a teacher, a friend, and a member of the community.*

Baptisms to Funerals

Christians also went to church to celebrate holidays, baptisms, marriages, and deaths. The first ritual, or religious ceremony, in a Christian's life was baptism. All Christian children were baptized a few days after they were born to show that they belonged to the Church. Couples were married at the church beginning in the 1140s and buried in the church's graveyard.

Centers of the Community

Churches were not only the center of religious life, they were places where friends met to chat or discuss village business. Schools were often in churches, markets were held outside the church, and some children even played ball games in churches when the weather was bad.

▼ *During a baptism, the priest either dipped the child into a special basin called a baptismal font or sprinkled the child with water as a symbol of washing away sin.*

Feast Days

In the Middle Ages, Christians celebrated holy days with special Masses, parades, and feasts. These holy days were known as Feast Days. Besides Sundays, they were often the only days when people did not have to work, which is where the word "holiday" comes from.

The main Christian holidays were Christmas, which celebrated the day Jesus was born, Easter, and Pentecost or Whitsunday. Pentecost took place on the seventh Sunday after Easter and remembered the day when Jesus' closest followers, the apostles, received a message to go out into the world and preach to others.

▲ *Peasants celebrate the Christmas season by singing Christmas carols and dancing.*

Christmas in the Middle Ages

In the Middle Ages, people decorated their homes for the Christmas season with ivy, bright-red holly berries, and mistletoe. Village ovens were in constant use baking breads and pies for the feast on Christmas Day, December 25. Some lords gave their servants gifts of clothing or money for Christmas, which people think is how the custom of giving presents at Christmastime began. People in the Middle Ages usually did not have to work from Christmas Day until **Epiphany**, twelve days later. They spent their holiday singing carols, acting in plays, and playing games.

◄ The Eucharist at Easter

Easter was the most important holy day of the Christian calendar. It was the one time of year when most medieval Christians over the age of twelve received the Eucharist. After Easter church service, people celebrated with a long walk in the countryside. During their walk, they chatted with one another, recited prayers, and sang religious songs. This long walk developed into the Easter parade, which still takes place today.

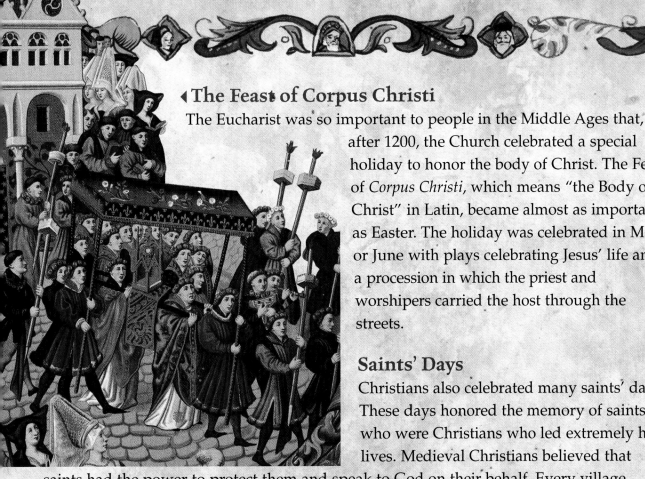

◀ The Feast of Corpus Christi

The Eucharist was so important to people in the Middle Ages that, after 1200, the Church celebrated a special holiday to honor the body of Christ. The Feast of *Corpus Christi*, which means "the Body of Christ" in Latin, became almost as important as Easter. The holiday was celebrated in May or June with plays celebrating Jesus' life and a procession in which the priest and worshipers carried the host through the streets.

Saints' Days

Christians also celebrated many saints' days. These days honored the memory of saints, who were Christians who led extremely holy lives. Medieval Christians believed that saints had the power to protect them and speak to God on their behalf. Every village, town, and city had a saint who watched over the community. On saints' days, Christians went to church to hear special prayers that honored the saint and to hear stories about the saint's life. Then, they gathered to watch a parade in which a statue of the saint was carried through the streets. They spent the rest of the day singing, dancing, eating, and drinking.

Mystery Plays

In the 1400s, groups of craftspeople and merchants in towns, called guilds, performed religious plays around the time of holy days. These plays, known as mystery plays, were based on stories from the Bible. By watching the plays, people who could not read learned Bible stories. At first, the plays were performed outside the church, but then they moved to marketplaces. In between plays, people bought food and drinks from vendors at stalls and talked with their friends.

Pilgrimages

Many Christians in the Middle Ages traveled great distances to visit churches and shrines that honored a saint. These travelers were called pilgrims, and their journeys, which were often very long and slow, were called pilgrimages. Pilgrims traveled by boat, on foot, by horseback, and in wagons, and faced many dangers along the way, including rough weather and robbers.

For some people, going on a pilgrimage was a way to show that they were good Christians while seeing other parts of the world. Priests sent people on pilgrimages as a way of asking God to forgive their sins. Other people visited pilgrimage sites to thank a saint for asking God to answer their prayers or to ask for a new favor, such as helping their crops grow. Pilgrims left gifts such as money, jewels, and candles to thank a saint for answering their prayers.

◀ *Many pilgrims prayed to saints to be cured of a disease. Some brought models of a body part they wished to be healed.*

Pilgrimage Sites

Many pilgrimage sites were in faraway places. Jerusalem, in present-day Israel, was where Jesus died. Rome, in Italy, was the home of the pope and the burial place of Saints Peter and Paul, two of Jesus' followers. Canterbury, in England, was where Thomas Becket, the archbishop of Canterbury, was buried.

So many pilgrims traveled to Santiago de Compostella, in northern Spain, to visit the grave of Saint James that inns and shops were set up along roads leading to the city. Pilgrims who traveled to Santiago de Compostella wore badges shaped like shells as souvenirs of their journey. Some pilgrims wrote guides that told other pilgrims where to stay and eat and what to see on the way. They also warned of robbers and other dangers. Most people could not afford to travel to these faraway places, so they visited holy places closer to home.

Relics

Many pilgrimage sites hold relics, or objects that belonged to a saint, such as a piece of clothing, a tooth, or a bone. People considered relics holy. They thought that by praying to the relics, the saint would speak to God on their behalf. Relics were kept in beautifully decorated cases that were sometimes made in the shape of the relic. A foot bone might be kept in a silver foot or a piece of skull in a container shaped like the saint's head. Relics were so valuable that some people stole them from one church and sold them to another.

A Gothic Cathedral

A cathedral is the main church of a diocese, where the bishop's throne, or "cathedra," is located. Cathedrals in the Middle Ages were beautiful stone buildings that were large enough to hold an entire city's population. They were meant to honor God and to show everyone who visited how important God was to the people of the city.

Early cathedrals were built in the Romanesque style, with thick walls, tiny windows, and massive pillars to support the roof. By 1150, **architects** were constructing cathedrals in the Gothic style. These buildings were so tall and filled with light that people felt they were looking up to heaven.

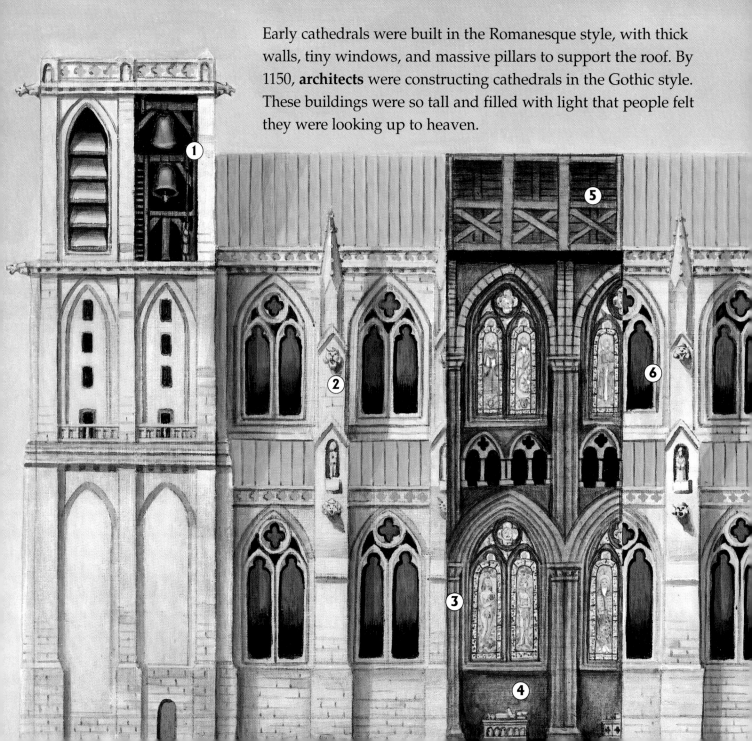

Parts of a Cathedral

1 Bronze bells, which called people to prayer, hung in bell towers.

2 Gargoyles looked like scary creatures, but they were really waterspouts that carried rainwater off the roof to the ground.

3 Piers were tall columns that supported arches and the roof.

4 Bishops were often buried in the cathedral in tombs placed in the aisles.

5 Ribbed vaulting helped support the enormous weight of the ceiling.

6 Pointed arches made people look toward heaven.

7 Flying buttresses were arches that helped support the walls.

8 The spire, like pointed arches, reached toward heaven.

9 Windows of colored glass showed stories from the Bible.

10 The clergy prayed in the choir.

11 The bishop performed Mass from the altar.

12 The apse often had small chapels where people prayed to saints.

Building Cathedrals

Building a cathedral or another large church was a major project that often took thousands of people and more than a hundred years to finish. Many cathedrals were never completed because there was not enough money.

A group of priests, known as the chapter, raised the money to pay for the cathedral. Wealthy people and guilds gave large gifts, while poorer people put a few pennies into collection boxes around the city. Those with no money offered to work on the cathedral for free.

The chapter hired an architect to design the cathedral. A master **mason** supervised its construction, which included hiring workers and arranging for building materials to be brought to the site.

▼ *Most work on a cathedral was done during the summer, when the weather was warm. During the colder months, laborers put up covers to protect the cathedral from wind, rain, and snow.*

Making Stained Glass

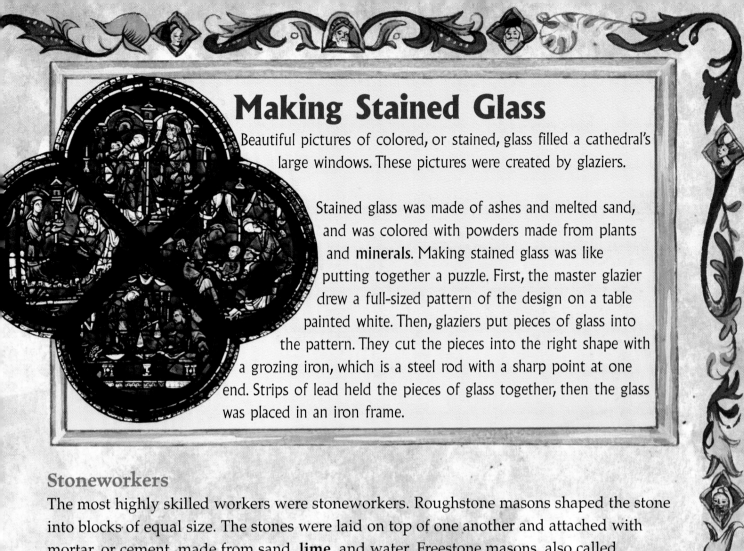

Beautiful pictures of colored, or stained, glass filled a cathedral's large windows. These pictures were created by glaziers.

Stained glass was made of ashes and melted sand, and was colored with powders made from plants and **minerals**. Making stained glass was like putting together a puzzle. First, the master glazier drew a full-sized pattern of the design on a table painted white. Then, glaziers put pieces of glass into the pattern. They cut the pieces into the right shape with a grozing iron, which is a steel rod with a sharp point at one end. Strips of lead held the pieces of glass together, then the glass was placed in an iron frame.

Stoneworkers

The most highly skilled workers were stoneworkers. Roughstone masons shaped the stone into blocks of equal size. The stones were laid on top of one another and attached with mortar, or cement, made from sand, **lime**, and water. Freestone masons, also called stonecutters or sculptors, did the more delicate carving work.

Many other craftspeople helped build the cathedral. Carpenters made wooden frames for arches and **timbers** for the roof. Plumbers made sheets of waterproof lead that covered the roof and frames that held pieces of stained glass. Blacksmiths made iron strips and nails to hold wooden beams together, and they made and repaired tools. Most workers did not have a special skill. They were laborers who carried construction materials and helped out wherever they were needed.

Christian Art

Cathedrals and other large churches contained stained glass windows, paintings, sculptures, and other works of art that were beautiful to look at and taught Christians about religion. Some medieval artists created frescoes, which were paintings done on walls made of plaster that was not quite dry. The paint combined with the moist plaster to create rich colors. Silk and wool tapestries hung on cathedral walls, telling stories from the Bible while keeping out drafts.

Sculptors carved scenes from the Bible on the outside walls of the cathedral in Amiens, France. In the Middle Ages, all the sculptures were painted in bright colors.

This fresco shows a scene from the Bible in which an angel visits three kings to tell them about the birth of Jesus Christ.

Labyrinths

Some Gothic cathedrals had labyrinths, which were like mazes, on the floor of their nave. The nave was the large open area where worshipers prayed. Christians who were not able to go on a pilgrimage because they were too sick, old, or poor walked through the labyrinth instead. Others crawled on their hands and knees as a form of penance for their sins.

Not all artwork in churches was serious. Sometimes, sculptors made funny carvings in places up high, where the bishop would not notice them. Pictures of mermaids, dragons, and animals were carved onto the bottom of hinged seats in the choir, where the clergy sang.

Art for Ceremonies

Skilled craftspeople made many beautiful works of art that were used in Christian ceremonies. The special clothes that the priest wore for Mass, called vestments, were made from the finest silks and were embroidered by skilled craftswomen. Other objects, such as monstrances and chalices, were made from gold, silver, ivory, and wood, and were decorated with jewels. A monstrance was used to display the host. The chalice held the wine used in the Eucharist ceremony. The chalice was supposed to look like the cup from which Jesus drank at the Last Supper, his final meal with his followers before being killed.

Monasteries

Some Christian men and women devoted their lives to God. They lived in special communities, called monasteries and convents, that were built around a large church where they prayed and studied. Men called monks were led by abbots. Women called nuns were led by abbesses.

Monasteries and convents were often built in remote places, so the monks and nuns would not be disturbed by the outside world. Some monasteries and convents became so well known as centers of study that towns grew up next to them.

Monks and nuns had to live by the rules of the monastery or convent. They were not allowed to own any personal possessions, they had to obey the abbot or abbess, and they were not allowed to have contact with anyone outside the monastery or convent without permission. They also prayed eight times each day, including once in the middle of the night.

▼ *The monastery of Mont Saint Michel, in France, was built on a rocky hill by the ocean. At high tide, the hill was surrounded by water. At low tide, when the ocean was far from shore, people walked to the monastery across the sand.*

Copying Texts

In the Middle Ages, before there were printing presses in Europe, books were copied by hand onto parchment, which was made from very thin pieces of sheepskin. Many monks and nuns worked as scribes, copying the books and decorating the pages with tiny, colorful paintings. The most expensive books, called illuminated manuscripts, sparkled with gold paint.

▶ *Monks and nuns copied texts in a special room called a scriptorium. The scriptorium was filled with desks, bookstands, and shelves where the books and tools used to copy them were stored.*

Caring for the Community

Monks and nuns took care of anyone who came to their communities for help. They gave food and clothing to the poor and took care of the elderly and sick in infirmaries, which were like hospitals. Pilgrims and other travelers stopped at monasteries and convents for food and a bed in the guesthouses. Sometimes, the monastery or convent had a school for local children.

Clothing

Monks and nuns wore simple clothing. A nun wore a long garment called a habit. A wimple covered her head and throat. A monk wore a plain woolen tunic with a long, loose, sleeveless garment, called a cowl, on top. The cowl had a deep hood to keep out distractions. Monks had a special hairstyle called the tonsure. They shaved the top of their heads, leaving just a short circle of hair above the ears.

▲ *Nuns ate together in a dining hall called a refectory. They were usually not allowed to talk during meals. Instead, they listened to a nun read to them from the Bible.*

Judaism

Judaism is the religion of the Jewish people and the religion from which Christianity grew. Jews believe in one God, and they follow his teachings, which are written in their holy book, the *Torah*.

During the Middle Ages, Jewish people lived in small communities in Christian and Muslim lands, where they quietly practiced their religion. The leader of the community was a rabbi, who was very knowledgeable about the *Torah*. He spent much of his time studying Jewish law and teaching others.

▲ *Rabbis in the Middle Ages studied the* **Talmud,** *which is a set of books that contains Jewish laws.*

▼ *A Jewish couple marries under a* **chupah,** *or canopy, made of shawls that men wear while they pray.*

Synagogues

The rabbi also led services in the synagogue, the Jewish house of worship. In the Middle Ages, synagogues were not only places of prayer and Jewish learning, but they were gathering places for the Jewish community.

Most synagogues were simple buildings that blended in with the buildings around them. The laws of the Christian and Muslim lands where Jews lived said that synagogues could not be taller or more beautiful than local churches or **mosques**.

The inside of a synagogue was also very simple. The walls were decorated with symbols of Judaism, such as the tablets of the Ten Commandments, the laws that God gave the **prophet** Moses. A great chest, called an ark, contained the *Torah* scrolls. The *bima*, or platform from which the rabbi led services, was usually in the center of the synagogue so that everyone could hear. Most synagogues had a separate prayer area for women.

▲ *During the Middle Ages, all Jews prayed three times a day — at dawn, in the late afternoon, and in the early evening.*

◄ *The Klausen Synagogue was built in the 1500s in Prague, in the Czech Republic. Jewish people have been buried in the synagogue's cemetery for hundreds of years.*

Islam

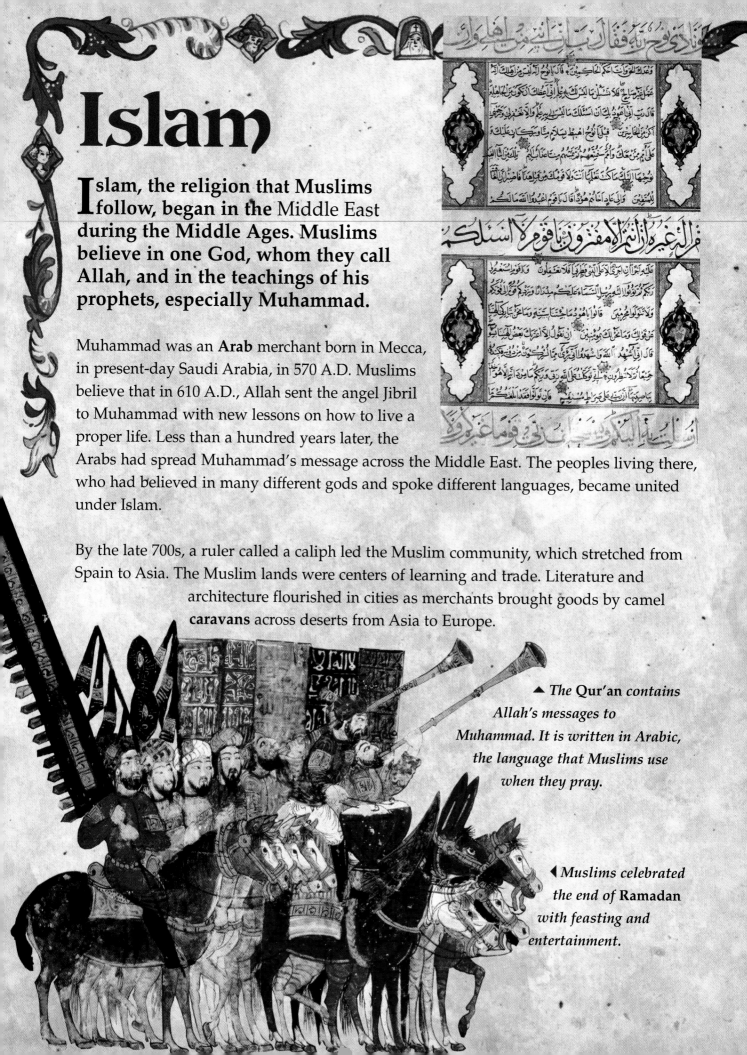

Islam, the religion that Muslims follow, began in the Middle East during the Middle Ages. Muslims believe in one God, whom they call Allah, and in the teachings of his prophets, especially Muhammad.

Muhammad was an **Arab** merchant born in Mecca, in present-day Saudi Arabia, in 570 A.D. Muslims believe that in 610 A.D., Allah sent the angel Jibril to Muhammad with new lessons on how to live a proper life. Less than a hundred years later, the Arabs had spread Muhammad's message across the Middle East. The peoples living there, who had believed in many different gods and spoke different languages, became united under Islam.

By the late 700s, a ruler called a caliph led the Muslim community, which stretched from Spain to Asia. The Muslim lands were centers of learning and trade. Literature and architecture flourished in cities as merchants brought goods by camel **caravans** across deserts from Asia to Europe.

▲ *The Qur'an contains Allah's messages to Muhammad. It is written in Arabic, the language that Muslims use when they pray.*

◀ *Muslims celebrated the end of **Ramadan** with feasting and entertainment.*

The Five Pillars of Islam

The most important teachings of Islam are called the Five Pillars of Islam. Muslims must pray five times a day facing the most important shrine in Mecca, the *ka'bah*. They must give charity to those in need and fast during the holy month of *Ramadan*, which celebrates the time when the angel Jibril first spoke to Muhammad. Finally, it is the duty of all Muslims to make a pilgrimage to Mecca, called the *hajj*, at least once in their lifetime if they are healthy and can afford the trip.

Muslim Law

Muslims also follow the *Shar'iah*, or Muslim law. The *Shar'iah* is a set of rules about all parts of life, including how a leader should rule, how to conduct business, how to treat a husband or wife, and what foods to eat.

▼ *Muslims bow in prayer facing Mecca to show their respect for Allah.*

Mosques

The mosque is the Muslim house of worship. In medieval times, it was also the main building of a Muslim town. Some mosques in the Middle Ages were plain, single-story buildings that had a minaret, or tower, from which a person known as a *muezzin* called worshipers to prayer. Other mosques were larger and more elaborate. They had several buildings, courtyards, towers, gateways, and domes.

Outside every mosque was a fountain where people washed their face, arms, hands, and feet before praying, and a place to leave their shoes before entering the mosque. Inside was a large, open space where the men knelt to pray on prayer rugs woven from wool, cotton, or silk. The women prayed in a separate area.

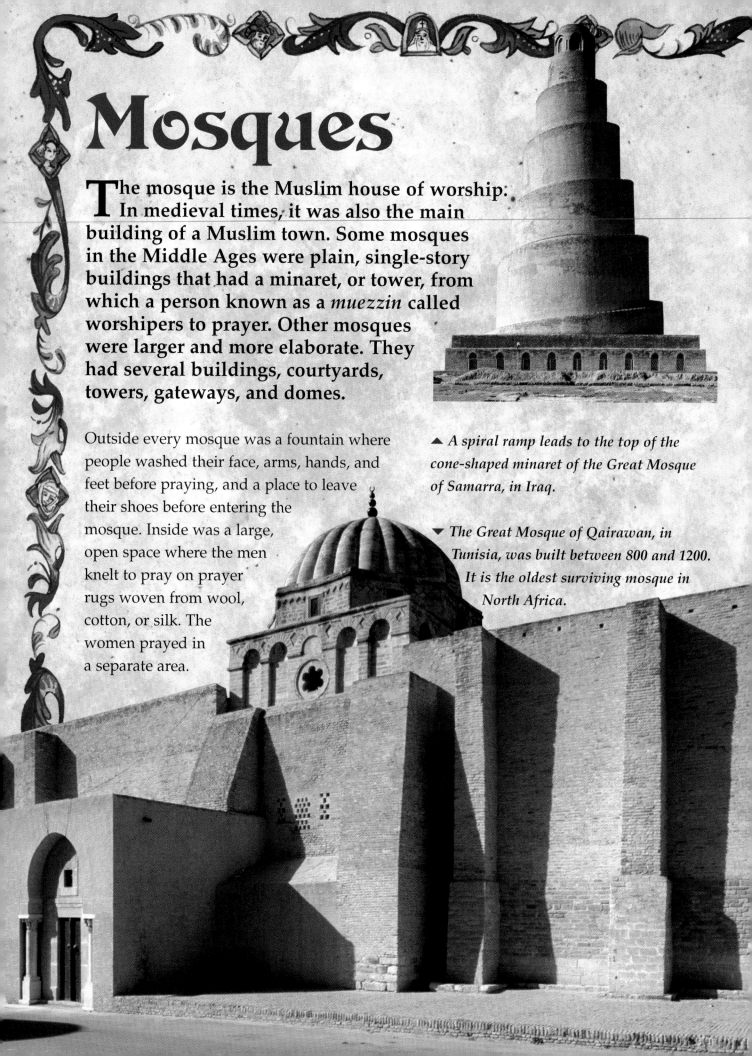

▲ *A spiral ramp leads to the top of the cone-shaped minaret of the Great Mosque of Samarra, in Iraq.*

▼ *The Great Mosque of Qairawan, in Tunisia, was built between 800 and 1200. It is the oldest surviving mosque in North Africa.*

Inside a Mosque

The *imam*, or leader of the community, led prayers from a platform called a *minbar*. The *minbar* was in front of a *mihrab*, a hollow in the wall that faced Mecca, the most holy city of Islam. The *mihrab* showed people in which direction to pray.

In the Middle Ages, many mosques were decorated with verses from the *Qur'an* written in beautiful writing called calligraphy, and with colorful tiles, **mosaics**, and metalwork in geometric designs.

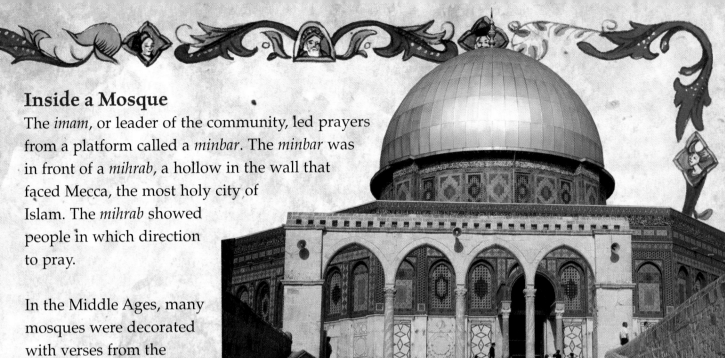

▼ *The Dome of the Rock, in Jerusalem, was built in 692 over the rock from which Muslims believe Muhammad rose to heaven one night to receive teachings from Allah.*

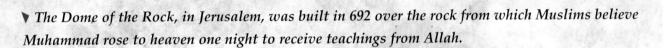

▼ *The Great Mosque of Cordoba, in Spain, was built in 785. The prayer hall is filled with almost 500 slender marble columns and striped arches, and the dome is decorated with beautiful mosaics.*

Heretics and Crusaders

During the Middle Ages, the Church believed that Christianity was the only true religion. People who followed other religions were forced to convert to Christianity, and were sometimes killed for refusing to give up their beliefs.

Heretics

The Catholic Church thought that some of its worst enemies were heretics. Heretics were people who started to follow religions that were like Catholicism but that did not include some of the major Catholic ideas. In the 1200s, the Church made special efforts to find and punish heretics. If people accused of being heretics did not confess or give up their beliefs, they were given penances, or punishments, were put in prison, or were tortured or killed.

Jews

Some medieval Christians blamed Jews for Jesus' death and considered Jews to be enemies of God. When there were accidents or disasters, such as famines or deadly diseases, they blamed the Jews, burned their communities, and killed them. In the 1200s, the Church passed a law saying that all Jews had to wear a yellow circle on their clothes or a yellow hat so that everyone knew they were Jewish. In the late 1200s and early 1300s, Jews were expelled, or sent away by force, from England and France. Then, in the late 1300s, Jews in some parts of Spain were forced to become Christians or killed.

▲ *Some heretics were punished by being burned alive.*

The Spanish Inquisition

In the 1400s, some people in Spain feared that former Jews, Muslims, and other non-Christians were still practicing their religion in secret. In 1481, the king and queen of Spain assembled a group of priests to punish non-Christians. This group formed a special court, known as the Spanish Inquisition, which tried and **executed** thousands of people or forced them to leave Spain.

▲ *A man is questioned at a trial during the Spanish Inquisition.*

The Crusades

Between 1096 and 1291, large armies of Christians fought a series of wars, known as the crusades, in the **Holy Land**. They were trying to recapture the land, which had special religious importance to Christians, Muslims, and Jews, from Muslims. Christians believed that Muslims were destroying Christian **sacred** places in the Holy Land and attacking Christian pilgrims traveling to Jerusalem. Over the next 200 years, many Muslims and Christians lost their lives fighting in the crusades.

▼ *The crusaders captured the holy city of Jerusalem from the Muslims in 1099. Muslims recaptured the city in 1187.*

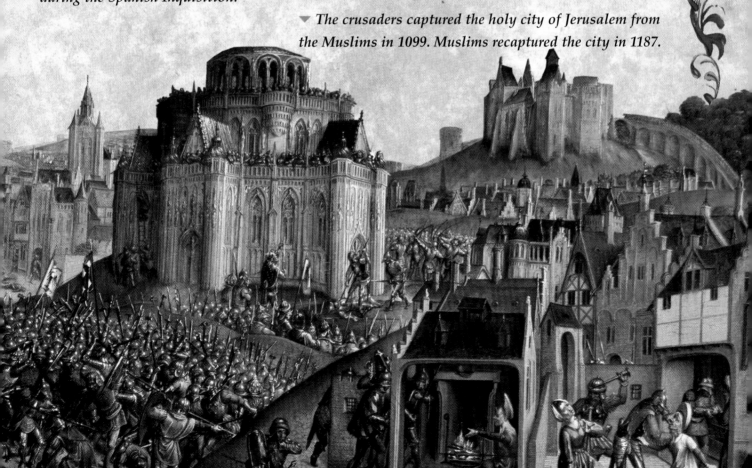

Religion Around the World

In other parts of the world, people in the Middle Ages worshiped many different gods and followed different religious traditions.

Hinduism

During the Middle Ages, many people in India and Southeast Asia followed the religion of Hinduism. Hindus believe that there is one supreme God called Brahman, but that thousands of gods and goddesses represent different parts of him. Hindus also believe that people are reincarnated, or born again and again after they die, until they are free from evil. Hindus in the Middle Ages worshiped at massive temples built by their rulers. When the rulers died, they were buried in the temples.

Angkor Wat, in what is now Cambodia, is the largest religious structure ever built. The temple complex was constructed in the 1100s to honor the Hindu god Vishnu and to show the closeness between the emperor and God.

The Aztecs

The Aztecs, in what is now central and southern Mexico, prayed to the gods of the sky, earth, corn, sun, and moon. They asked the gods for help in their daily life, for example, making their crops grow and winning battles against their enemies. The Aztecs built large temples on top of enormous stone **pyramids** where they **sacrificed** prisoners to their gods. The Aztecs believed that their gods, especially the sun god, Huitzilopochtli, would die without human blood to keep them strong.

▷ *Aztec priests offered their gods the hearts of enemies captured in war, then threw the prisoners' bodies down the temple steps.*

Buddhism

Many people in India, China, Japan, and parts of Indonesia followed the religion of Buddhism in the Middle Ages. Buddhism is based on the teachings of Siddhartha Gautama, who is known as "the Buddha," or "the Enlightened One." Buddhists believe that people are reincarnated and that what they are in the next life depends on how they acted in their last life. In the Middle Ages, the most devoted followers of the teachings of the Buddha were monks and nuns who gave up their possessions and lived in monasteries. They shaved their heads, wore robes of orange cloth, and followed strict rules written in the *Vinaya Sutra*, one of the three Buddhist holy books.

The Buddhist temple of Borobudur is on the island of Java, in Indonesia. It was built of black volcanic rock around 800 A.D. by hundreds of sculptors, painters, plasterers, and master masons. Borobudur is shaped like a ten-stepped pyramid. The sides of each step are covered with carvings that tell about the life of the Buddha and about everyday life in medieval Java.

Glossary

Arab A person from the Middle East

archbishop The most powerful bishop

architect A person who designs buildings

caravan A group traveling together, usually with camels

cathedral A very large church

convert To change religion

devil An evil spirit believed to be God's enemy

emperor A ruler of a country or group of countries

Epiphany A holy day that celebrates the visit of three kings to the baby Jesus Christ

execute To kill someone as punishment

famine A serious shortage of food in a large area

Holy Land An area in present-day Israel, Jordan, and Syria that has special religious meaning for Christians, Muslims, and people of other religions

lime A white powdery chemical

mason A person who builds with stone or brick

Mass The main ceremony of the Roman Catholic Church

merchant A person who buys and sells goods

Middle East A region in southwest Asia and northern Africa

mineral A substance obtained through mining

mosaic An artistic pattern made with small pieces of glass, tile, or stone

mosque A building in which Muslims pray

noble A person born into a ruling class

plaster A mixture of lime, water, and sand used to cover walls and ceilings

preach To give a religious speech to teach others

prophet A person believed to carry a message from God

pyramid A stone structure with a flat square base and flat triangular sides that meet in a point

sacred Having special religious meaning

sacrifice To offer a living thing to a god as an act of worship

shrine A small area or structure dedicated to a god or saint

sin To think or act in a way that goes against God's wishes

tapestry A woven piece of cloth hung as decoration on walls

timber Wood used to create furniture, buildings, and other objects

torture To injure or hurt someone on purpose

Index

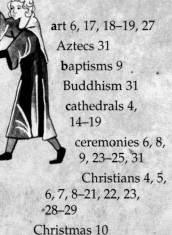

1 2 3 4 5 6 7 8 9 0   Printed in the U.S.A.   8 7 6 5 4 3